Who Was Chuck Jones?

by Jim Gigliotti

illustrated by John Hinderliter

Penguin Workshop
An Imprint of Penguin Random House

For Joycelyn, because "you're so wovewy"—JG

For Nathan, because a creative life is the best life
—JH

PENGUIN WORKSHOP
Penguin Young Readers Group
An Imprint of Penguin Random House LLC

Text copyright © 2017 by Jim Gigliotti. Illustrations copyright © 2017 by Penguin Random House LLC. All rights reserved. Published by Penguin Workshop, an imprint of Penguin Random House LLC, 345 Hudson Street, New York, New York 10014. PENGUIN and PENGUIN WORKSHOP are trademarks of Penguin Books Ltd. WHO HQ & Design is a registered trademark of Penguin Random House LLC. Printed in the USA.

Library of Congress Cataloging-in-Publication Data is available.

ISBN 9780448488578 (paperback)   10 9 8 7 6 5 4 3 2 1
ISBN 9780515159172 (library binding)   10 9 8 7 6 5 4 3 2 1

Contents

Who Was Chuck Jones?

Chuck Jones was eight years old and living in Ocean Park, California, when a stray cat named Johnson walked up the sand to his back doorstep one summer day in 1921.

Chuck had never seen the skinny, short-haired cat before. He called him Johnson, because that was the name written on a small, wooden tag around the cat's neck. Chuck liked Johnson, and Johnson  liked Chuck. So Johnson decided—as anyone with a cat knows, it was Johnson's idea—to stay with the Jones family for a little while.

Chuck laughed when Johnson would bat a grapefruit into a corner of the house, trapping it so he could bite into it and get at the juicy inside. And he laughed when Johnson would jump into the ocean and climb onto the shoulders of an unsuspecting swimmer. And when Johnson, covered in bits of tar and seagull feathers, surprised a group of sunbathers on the beach one day.

By watching Johnson, Chuck realized that animals have their own personalities, just like humans do. And he realized that it was the unexpected things in life that made people laugh.

When Chuck grew up to direct cartoons, he often used animals to tell his stories. And not just any animals, but some of the most famous cartoon animals ever created: Bugs Bunny, Daffy Duck, the Road Runner, Wile E. Coyote, Pepé Le Pew, Michigan J. Frog, and many more. His characters starred in short cartoons and feature-length cartoons, television shows and movies.

What made Chuck's cartoon characters so memorable was that each had its own special personality, just like Johnson. And each behaved in surprising ways, just like Johnson. A rabbit sang opera. A skunk fell in love with a cat, a frog broke into a song-and-dance routine—and a coyote tried all sorts of crazy ways to catch a roadrunner in the desert. And they all made people laugh. Many of Chuck's creations have entertained children and adults for more than fifty years!

CHAPTER 1
Growing Up in California

When Chuck Jones was a youngster, he loved stories. Chuck grew up before most people had radios and before television existed. But he enjoyed reading interesting books. He delighted in hearing the fantastic tales his relatives told. And he liked watching people act out funny performances onstage and in the movies.

Chuck was born Charles Martin Jones in Spokane, Washington, on September 21, 1912. His father's name also was Charles. His mother's name was Mabel. His oldest sister, Margaret, was born in 1908. Another sister, Dorothy, was born in 1910. Chuck's father worked at many different jobs. When he first met Mabel in 1906, he worked for a railroad company. That company sent him to Panama for a while to help work on the Panama Canal. Margaret and Dorothy were born in Panama, but the family moved back to the United States—to Spokane, Washington—

shortly before Chuck was born. The family moved to southern California in 1913, when Chuck was about six months old. Chuck's younger brother, Richard, was born two years later.

Chuck's father wanted to open and run his own business. He had many different ideas about how to get started. Unfortunately, none of his businesses were very successful. He tried buying and selling land, growing flowers, even selling avocados, but nothing seemed to work out quite right.

Every time Chuck's father started a new business, he ordered nice pencils and good paper on which he printed the name of his company. And every time the new company failed, he had stacks of paper and boxes of pencils left over.

Since they all had the company name on them,
they were no longer of any use to Mr. Jones.
He always gave the paper and the pencils to his
children. Chuck and his siblings usually had the
best paper and the most pencils of any kids in
their neighborhood. And they put it all to good
use! Chuck drew at least twenty pictures every day

for as long as he could remember. He was getting good at it, too. "Chuck's talent began to show at a very early age," his brother later said.

Mabel encouraged her children to draw. She would never criticize their drawings, but she never praised them unless she really meant it, either. Instead, she just let them have fun with their artwork. "It was a happy experience to draw for the joy of drawing," Chuck said.

The Jones family moved several times throughout southern California. They lived in and around the Hollywood area and sometimes out by the beach. Wherever the family moved, Chuck's father made sure that they rented a house that came with furniture and books already in place. "And not just any books," Chuck said, "but good books." To Chuck's father, that meant books by famous authors such as Charles Dickens, Mark Twain, and O. Henry. Mr. Jones thought that reading was very important.

In fact, conversation was not permitted at breakfast—only reading was allowed. If one of the Jones children forgot to bring a book to the table, he or she could read the cereal box!

So Chuck learned to read by the time he was three years old. As he grew, he went through all the good books in all their different houses, and the not-so-good ones, too.

When Chuck wasn't reading, he listened to his uncle Lynn tell stories. Uncle Lynn told some pretty crazy tales. Sometimes they were just silly,

like one about a zebra whose stripes had slipped off his back. At other times, the stories helped the kids feel better. When Teddy, the Jones family dog, died, Uncle Lynn said that the dog had called him to say he was okay. Uncle Lynn wasn't entirely sure where Teddy was calling from, but he thought it might have been from Dog Heaven.

On some weekends, Chuck and Richard would visit Uncle Kent, who sold cars in downtown Los Angeles. Uncle Kent always gave the boys money to see a live vaudeville show. Vaudeville had many different performers onstage, one after another. The first might be an acrobat, and the next a singer. Chuck liked the comedians best. He always enjoyed their funny skits and jokes.

Chuck learned a lot about comedy from watching the vaudeville acts. And he learned from watching silent movies, too. When Chuck was about six years old, his family moved to a house on Sunset Boulevard in Hollywood. The house was only a couple of blocks away from where movie star Charlie Chaplin built his own studio in 1918. Chuck sometimes sat outside and saw famous stars such as Chaplin or Mary Pickford or Lloyd Hamilton—the greatest stars of the silent movies—going to or from work. This was almost a decade before "talking pictures"—movies with sound—were invented.

Charlie Chaplin (1889–1977)

Comic actor Charlie Chaplin was one of the earliest movie stars—and he's still one of the most famous performers of all time.

Chaplin was born in London. He began his career on the stage in England when he was just a child. In 1914 he started acting in silent films in the United States. Chaplin was an instant hit as a comedian in silent films, and his character "the Tramp"—with his little mustache, funny walk, and bowler hat—is still recognized around the world.

Chaplin soon began writing and directing films, in addition to starring in them. In 1919, he helped form the United Artists movie company. He worked as a movie director and producer for nearly fifty years after that. In 1972, he was presented with an Honorary Academy Award for his lifetime contributions to the movies.

Chuck went to the movies and saw how funny Chaplin was. He laughed at common, everyday things, like the funny way Chaplin walked.

Chuck's dad told him that Charlie Chaplin once filmed a scene 132 times until he got it just right. Chuck wondered if that was true. And he wondered if a zebra's stripes could ever really fall down around its ankles.

CHAPTER 2
On to Art School

One of the houses in which Chuck lived when he was growing up included a collection of books by Mark Twain. Chuck read through the entire collection. One of the books was called *Roughing It*—the story of a pair of brothers who cross the United States in a stagecoach. Chuck read the book over and over. What he remembered most about it was Twain's detailed description of a coyote.

Mark Twain (1835–1910)

Mark Twain is the pen name of the American author and humorist who wrote *The Adventures of Tom Sawyer* and *Adventures of Huckleberry Finn*. Twain—whose real name was Samuel Clemens—first became famous for "The Celebrated Jumping Frog of Calaveras County," a short story written in 1865. By the end of his career, he had written twenty-eight books and many short stories and essays. Twain was in great demand as a public speaker, and he became one of the most famous men in the world.

Mark Twain had described the coyote in *Roughing It* as being thin and scrawny, with funny-looking hair. Chuck thought that sounded like a pretty accurate description of himself. Chuck was so skinny in high school, he imagined that other people could see him only by looking straight at him, but not from the side! He was six foot one and weighed only 125 pounds.

Chuck wasn't confident about his looks. And he didn't like school. He didn't feel like he fit in.

And although he was very smart, having read so much as a child, he was bored. Chuck earned good grades in the classes he liked, but he let his imagination roam in others.

Before his junior year, his father took Chuck out of high school and enrolled him at Chouinard (say: shuh-NARD) Art Institute in Los Angeles. (It's now called the California Institute of the Arts, or sometimes just CalArts.) That was okay with Chuck. He would call it his "great, good luck" to leave high school for art school.

Chouinard Art Institute

On Chuck's first day at Chouinard, one of his teachers told the students that they all had a hundred thousand bad drawings in them—meaning they all would draw plenty of bad pictures before they learned to draw any good ones. That was okay with Chuck, too. He felt that he'd been drawing for so long that he already was on his second batch of one hundred thousand bad drawings!

A teacher named Don Graham taught Chuck to develop his own style and work his way toward creating those good drawings. While students worked on their drawings, Graham did not praise or criticize. Instead, he asked, "Having fun?" (for good work) or "Having problems?" (for not-so-good work). "I would rather hear Don Graham say, 'Having fun?' than win an academic award," Chuck said.

Chuck sometimes looked around at the other students and felt as if they were all pretty good artists—and he wasn't. Or, as he complained to Uncle Lynn one day after school, "You can't make a racehorse out of a pig!" That was true, Uncle Lynn wisely told him, "but you can make a very fast pig."

In other words, he couldn't try to be something that he wasn't. "I realized that was what it was all about," Chuck later said. There was no point in comparing himself to other students. Whatever Chuck decided to do with his life, he could only try to be the best that he could be.

Chuck worked hard during his time at Chouinard. At two o'clock each morning, he would take a bus to work as a janitor cleaning a nearby office building. After four hours of work, he went to his classes. When his school day ended, he also cleaned at Chouinard to help pay his tuition.

Like most of his classmates, Chuck hoped to become a famous artist one day. He dreamed of moving to Paris and creating famous paintings. But when Chuck graduated in 1931, it was difficult for anybody to find work—especially someone just getting out of school and with little experience. At the time, the United States was in the midst of the Great Depression. Many people lost their jobs and their homes and their life savings. Chuck had no idea how he was going to make a living after art school.

Chapter 3
The Working World

Ub Iwerks

Not long after Chuck graduated from Chouinard, a friend from school called to tell him that Ub Iwerks was hiring people to work at his animation studio. Iwerks was the animator who had created Mickey Mouse just three years earlier, while working with Walt Disney.

Iwerks had animated famous early Mickey Mouse cartoons such as *Steamboat Willie* and *Skeleton Dance*, but he had since opened his own business. Fortunately for Chuck, the movie industry wasn't as hurt by the Great Depression as most industries had been. People still wanted to go to the movies.

Chuck was only eighteen years old when he was hired by Ub Iwerks in 1931. Art school had prepared Chuck well for a career in animation—even though he didn't realize it at the time. The thousands of drawings he did in art school were like practice for creating all the drawings needed for a short cartoon. Drawing was what Chuck liked to do most, and what he was good at. Now, someone was going to pay him to do it. "Imagine that!" he later said, and called it "the most incredible thing that ever happened in the history of my life."

Movie Shorts

From the 1920s through the 1950s, the price of a movie ticket included the feature film and several short films such as comedies, cartoons, and newsreels. Movie "shorts" were usually under ten minutes long and shown before the regular movie or in between the two movies of a double feature.

By the mid-1950s, television had become quite popular. Movie shorts became a thing of the past. Because cartoon "shorts" had been created on film, they survived to be shown over and over again on television.

But Chuck didn't start off as an animator—an artist—right away. He had to work his way up from the bottom. And in those days, the bottom of the animation ladder was a cel washer.

A cel (the name was derived from *celluloid*) was a hard, transparent, plastic material on which drawings for animation were made. Cels were expensive. They cost about seven cents each when

Chuck started with Iwerks, and a seven-minute cartoon might need tens of thousands of cels. Studios reused cels to save money. It was much less expensive to pay someone like Chuck about fifteen dollars a week to wash the old drawings off cels and reuse them instead of buying new ones each time.

After six months as a cel washer, Chuck moved up to cel painter and then cel inker. Next, he became an in-betweener—drawing the frames in between the main images that were already done by the animators. Chuck worked for more than a year for Iwerks, and he spent time at other studios, too. But Iwerks was struggling to make a profit—and in 1933 Chuck was fired, he said, by a secretary named Dorothy Webster.

Chuck needed to find another job. He thought he would become a janitor once again. Then a friend from Chouinard opened a small bookstore on Olvera Street in downtown Los Angeles.

How Animation Works

Traditional animation—the kind that is hand-drawn—was standard before computers were used. It is a long process with many steps.

- It starts, of course, with a story. Once a story is approved, a script is written and the actors' voices are recorded. (This is done first because animators match their drawings to the spoken words, not the other way around.)

- Animators then make the most important drawings for each scene. An "in-betweener" fills in the less important drawings using the exact same style for each character and scene.

- Once all the drawings in a scene have been made, an inker copies the outline of the drawing onto a transparent cel. Then a painter fills in the colors of the character on the back side of the cel. Putting colors on the back side makes the character look sharper. Other artists have painted the backgrounds on separate cels.

- The cels are then photographed to create each image—frame—of the film. With twelve to twenty-four frames making up a single second, it requires thousands of cels to make a seven-minute movie.

The director of an animated film oversees every step of the process, working with the team he or she has assembled. With all the effort and expense that

goes into producing a single scene, the director has to get it right the first time. Unlike a live-action movie, there are no second takes!

Olvera Street is a Mexican-style marketplace in the oldest part of downtown Los Angeles. It has many people who sell food, crafts, and clothing—and it attracts many tourists. Chuck's friend asked him to draw portraits near his bookstore's entrance in the hopes that it would bring tourists into the shop. Chuck charged one dollar per portrait.

Chuck didn't think he drew people's faces very well, because he had trouble getting the eyes right. But he felt he could draw them reasonably well in profile—that is, from the side. He would simply try to make everyone look pretty.

"They'd go away happy, and I'd get my dollar!" he said. Chuck liked his work outside the bookstore. He enjoyed talking to people.

Sometimes he earned a little extra money by helping the puppeteers on Olvera Street. The expert puppeteers taught him important lessons about the characters they controlled. If the marionettes' knees bent or their feet weren't planted solidly on the ground, for instance, the performance looked sloppy.

Chuck learned a lot about the right way for the marionettes to move. It was good practice for his career in animation.

As enjoyable and as valuable as it was to work
on Olvera Street, Chuck wasn't making enough
money to pay his bills. Besides, he was in love,
and thinking about getting married and starting a
family. His bride-to-be was Dorothy Webster, the
same secretary who had fired him from Iwerks's
studio!

In 1933, Dorothy helped Chuck find a job with a movie studio called Leon Schlesinger Productions. Chuck began as an in-betweener at the new studio. And he and Dorothy were married in 1935. Two years later, Dorothy gave birth to their baby daughter, Linda.

Chuck had a good job and a family. He was beginning a new chapter in his life.

CHAPTER 4
"What's Up, Doc?"

Chuck continued to climb the animation ladder. In 1938, when he was just twenty-five years old, he became the youngest animation supervisor for Leon Schlesinger Productions. His days of washing cels were over. He had become a director.

At Schlesinger Productions, Chuck worked on Looney Tunes and Merrie Melodies cartoons for Warner Bros. Pictures, which bought Leon Schlesinger Productions in 1944. Merrie Melodies and Looney Tunes were two series of funny short films produced from the early 1930s until the end of the 1960s— an era known as the Golden Age of Animation.

They both had been named after Walt Disney Productions' Silly Symphonies, but they would become more popular than Disney's, or any other competitor's, cartoons.

Each Merrie Melodies cartoon originally ended with the line, "So Long, Folks!" and each Looney Tunes cartoon with the line, "That's All, Folks!" But by 1936, all the films for both series ended the same way: "That's all Folks!" They also came to share the theme music: a 1937 song called "The Merry-Go-Round Broke Down."

Chuck worked with a creative group of people in the animation department. They had a lot of fun at their jobs, because the Warner Bros. bosses were not often around. One writer, Cal Howard, ran a hot dog stand out of his desk! Another acted as the lookout near the front entrance. If he saw one of their bosses coming, he would push a button under his desk that activated lights at

the other employees' desks. Everyone quickly tried to look busy.

Cal Howard delivered hot dogs to other floors in a basket that was pulled up and down by a rope on the outside of the building. One time, someone opened a window and used a metal hook to grab the basket and steal the food.

The next time, Cal put a firecracker in the basket. No more stolen hot dogs!

The Schlesinger animators worked in a building that was not near the main Warner Bros. studio and offices. The people who worked there called the Schlesinger building "Termite Terrace" because it was so old and in need of repair—and also because of all the termites.

Despite the condition of the building, the remote location had a good side: Chuck forged a close and creative working relationship with the other directors at Termite Terrace.

Frank Tashlin   Friz Freleng   Tex Avery

He learned about making cartoons from animators such as Tex Avery, Friz Freleng, and Frank Tashlin. And he learned the importance of working together as a team.

Chuck Jones

Tex Avery (1908–1980)

Fred "Tex" Avery was a legendary animator best known for his work with characters such as Bugs Bunny, Porky Pig, and Chilly Willy. He worked for Leon Schlesinger Productions from 1935 to 1941, then later for Metro-Goldwyn-Mayer (MGM) and other studios. His nickname came from his hometown of Taylor, Texas.

When Avery attended North Dallas High School, a common greeting among friends was, "What's

up, Doc?" He added that to his first Bugs Bunny cartoon, *A Wild Hare*, in 1940, and it became the rabbit's most famous line.

The first feature Chuck directed was called *The Night Watchman* in 1938. *The Night Watchman* features Tommy Cat, who tries to make sure the mice don't misbehave one night while his father (the regular night watchman) is out sick. Of course, the mice do misbehave. They take advantage of Tommy Cat until he fights back.

The Night Watchman was fun to watch and had moments of charm, but it wasn't great. Instead, *The Night Watchman* was a learning experience for Chuck. "You have to stumble a lot," he said. "I can't think of any other way of doing anything. There are no short-cuts."

Like *The Night Watchman*, much of Chuck's early work included gentle characters that were as realistic as possible—or, at least, as realistic as talking animals can be! They might make people smile but not really laugh. Chuck was imitating the formula that had worked for Walt Disney in creating his characters, which included a character called Sniffles, a cute mouse drawn in the Mickey Mouse style. "I didn't know anything else to do but study the people who came before me," Chuck said later.

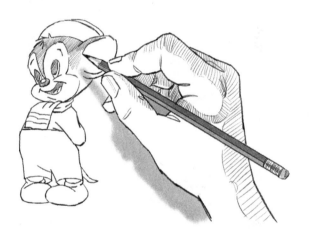

In the 1940s, however, Chuck began to break away from the Disney formula and develop his own style of storytelling. A major turning point was *The Draft Horse* in 1942. World War II was in full swing by then.

The United States had entered the war after Pearl Harbor in Hawaii was bombed in December 1941.

Chuck directed a cartoon about a horse that rushes to enlist in the army. The horse gets rejected and ends up knitting sweaters for soldiers. Chuck gave the horse a wacky personality and an energy not seen in his earlier films.

When Chuck watched *The Draft Horse* in a theater, he was delighted to hear people laughing

out loud. "Once you have heard a strange audience burst into laughter at a film you directed, you realize what the word *joy* is all about," he said later.

Chuck had discovered what he was best at. From then on, his stories wouldn't just give people a smile or a little chuckle here and there. They would make people roar with laughter.

CHAPTER 5
The Bugs Bunny in Me

Not long after directing a cartoon about a horse that wanted to join the army, Chuck began directing cartoons for people who really *were* in the army. These cartoons served as training films for US soldiers. They were funny films, but they served a serious purpose: to keep soldiers safe by teaching them the right way to do things.

From 1943 to 1945, Chuck directed twelve of the twenty-six training films that Warner Bros. made for the US Army. Many of them were written by Theodor Geisel, an author better known as Dr. Seuss. World War II training films covered topics such as firing a weapon or driving a tank. But some were not about fighting the war at all. The army wanted Warner Bros. to make animated films because they knew that cartoons would be a funny way to get important points across.

Chuck's military cartoons featured a young army man named Private Snafu. *SNAFU* is an old military acronym that stands for "Situation Normal: All Fouled Up."

Private Snafu does everything wrong. He goofs off instead of studying maps and charts. He doesn't protect himself from disease-carrying mosquitoes. Every time he does something wrong, he puts himself and other soldiers in danger. By showing the men and women of the armed forces the wrong way to do things—in a funny manner—Chuck taught them the *right* way to do things.

The Private Snafu cartoons let Chuck try things he normally wouldn't have. Free from studio executives saying "No!" he took risks that he never did at his studio job. And the men and women of the military thought Private Snafu was hilarious. The films were important for Chuck, because they gave him the courage to be bolder in his regular films.

Chuck became more daring with Bugs Bunny—and gave him the personality that made Bugs such a favorite—with *Super-Rabbit* in 1943. By then, Bugs already had appeared in cartoons with several different directors. And just like with real-life actors, cartoon characters have a different personality when working with different directors.

In *Super-Rabbit*, "you could see that he [Bugs] was really enjoying himself, which I enjoyed,"

Chuck said. "It was a matter of understanding the Bugs Bunny in me."

Super-Rabbit is based on the Superman cartoon series. Bugs battles a villain named Cottontail Smith who is trying to eliminate all rabbits. Just when Cottontail is about to get Bugs, the super-rabbit emerges from a phone booth in the uniform of a "real Superman," a member of the US Marine Corps.

Bugs has fun with Cottontail without ever being mean, and he is clearly enjoying himself. Fighting the bad guy is just a game for him. The cartoon ends with Bugs telling Cottontail and his horse, "Sorry, fellas, I can't play with you anymore. I've got important work to do." And he marches off to the battlefields of World War II.

Chuck said Bugs was who he wanted to be: stylish, funny, and always quick with a clever comeback line. "My admiration for Bugs is immeasurable," he once wrote. He would come home from work and tell his wife, Dorothy, the things that Bugs did that day, as if the cartoon character was a real person.

The character of Bugs Bunny *was* real to many other people, too. Once, Chuck was introduced to a little boy as the man who drew Bugs Bunny. "He doesn't draw Bugs Bunny," the boy insisted. "He draws *pictures* of Bugs Bunny."

When one of the men who wrote for Chuck explained his job to his own grandmother, she said, "I can't understand why you're writing scripts for Bugs Bunny. He's funny enough just as he is."

While Chuck was hard at work on the Bugs Bunny cartoons, he was also creating

his own characters for Looney Tunes. In 1945, he created Pepé Le Pew—a French skunk who is always looking for love, usually with a cat who does not feel the same way about him.

Chuck saw the wishful side of himself in Pepé. He remembered being shy and uncertain around girls when he was younger. But Pepé was

confident. "Pepé always represented the other side of my personality," Chuck said, "because he represented what I wanted to be, and what I think every man would like to be: irresistible."

PEPÉ LE PEW in
"Two Scents Worth"
A MERRIE MELODIE CARTOON
A WARNER BROS CARTOON

Pepé was usually rejected by the cats he chased because, well, he was a skunk! Still, it never stopped him from trying. He appeared in seventeen cartoons starting in 1945, with all but three of them directed by Jones.

Pepé was Chuck's most famous creation to date. But Chuck soon would reach back to his childhood memories to create two even bigger stars.

CHAPTER 6
"Beep! Beep!"

In 1949, Chuck came up with two of his best-known characters. He thought back to the coyote Mark Twain described in *Roughing It*. What would a coyote like to eat for dinner, he thought? Maybe a roadrunner, if he was fast enough to catch one. The Road Runner and Wile E. Coyote were born. (Say

(CARNIVERUS VULGARIS)

"Wile E." fast: It sounds like *wily*, which means "clever.")

Chuck came up with the idea for the Road Runner's sound from background artist Paul

Julian. One day, Paul was walking down the hallway at Warner Bros. with some drawings. They were stacked so high that he couldn't see over them. "Beep, beep!" Paul called out so he wouldn't run into anybody. "Beep, beep!" Chuck asked Paul to be the voice of the Road Runner.

The Road Runner and the Coyote appeared
in twenty-six cartoons directed by Chuck over
the next sixteen years, beginning with *Fast and
Furry-ous*. (Other directors also worked with the
characters after that.) The formula was always the
same: The Road Runner runs along the desert
highway. The Coyote tries to catch Road Runner,
but his clever tricks *always* backfire. He never
catches Road Runner, but the Coyote does injure
himself—a lot. The Road Runner occasionally
startles him with a well-timed "Beep, beep!"

before racing away. In fact, those are the only words that are ever said in the entire series of the

Road Runner and Coyote cartoons!

In 1950, the same year that the Road Runner and Coyote first appeared, two cartoons directed by Chuck won Academy Awards—a huge honor for anyone in the movie industry.

For Scent-imental Reasons, starring Pepé Le Pew, won the award for Best Animated Short Film. Chuck's *So Much for So Little* won for Best Documentary Short Subject. *So Much for So Little* was a cartoon Chuck directed for the US government's Public Health Service.

So Much for So Little

It encouraged better health care for babies, and it was the first time that an Academy Award for a documentary was awarded to an animated film.

The ACME Corporation

Wile E. Coyote tries to catch the Road Runner with an assortment of wacky products that he orders from the ACME Corporation. *Acme* comes from a Greek word that means the very best of something—literally, the "highest point." But the ACME Corporation's products are anything but the best. They always backfire on the Coyote just when he thinks he is closing in on the Road Runner.

Some of the ACME products that *almost* help the Coyote trap his dinner include an anvil, rocket-powered roller skates, a tornado kit, a giant rubber band, an instant icicle maker, and a rocket-powered sled.

The ACME Corporation was completely made up, although there are real companies that use the name. In the early 1900s, the Sears, Roebuck catalog sold several Acme products—including an anvil!

Throughout the 1950s, Chuck continued to create even more memorable animal characters, each with a unique personality and character. Marc Antony was a huge bulldog who fiercely protected a cuddly kitten in *Feed the Kitty* (1952). Michigan J. Frog wore a top hat and carried a cane while dancing and singing in *One Froggy Evening* (1955). Such animals came from the memories Chuck had of his childhood. He remembered the funny way animals, like Johnson the grapefruit-loving cat, acted. "Early experiences convinced me that animals can and do have quite distinct personalities," he said.

Just as important, Chuck brought new and special personalities to already-existing Warner Bros. characters, such as Daffy Duck. Under Chuck's direction, Daffy became the exact opposite of Bugs Bunny. While Bugs was confident and self-assured, Daffy was uncertain and fearful that everyone was out to get him.

Duck Amuck (1953) is Chuck's most famous work with Daffy Duck. In it, an unseen artist frustrates Daffy by constantly changing the scenery, sound effects, and costumes. Sometimes, the illustrator's pencil erases Daffy, or leaves him with only a face, or even just a mouth.

At the end, the artist—the animator of the cartoon—is revealed to be Bugs Bunny. "Gee, ain't I a stinker?" Bugs says into the camera. The real "stinker" behind the scenes, of course, was Chuck.

"If anyone is going to be an animated cartoon director," he said, "they have to have the courage to reach down inside themselves and pull a character up to the surface and become that character."

CHAPTER 7
Beyond Warner Bros.

Except for a few months when he briefly worked at Disney Studios, Chuck remained with Warner Bros. until the early 1960s.

In 1962, he teamed with his wife, Dorothy, to write a full-length animated musical, *Gay Purr-ee*. Chuck had always delighted in Dorothy's "beauty, curiosity, and sense of wonder." He also described their child, Linda, as the "perfect daughter." Like everyone else at the time, Linda had grown up watching her dad's cartoons in movie theaters. Her favorite was Daffy Duck.

After leaving Warner Bros., Chuck helped form an animation company that did work for MGM Studios, including new  cartoons for the popular Tom and Jerry series. He also formed Chuck Jones Enterprises, which made animated specials for television, and produced and directed an award-winning animated film for MGM called *The Dot and the Line*. Subtitled "A Romance in Lower Mathematics," *The Dot and the Line* was based on a children's book of the same name by Norton Juster.

The story is about a land in which the women were all dots and the men were all lines. A straight male line was in love with a female dot, but couldn't get her to notice him. Instead, the female dot hung out with a wild, squiggly line. When the straight line discovered different shapes he could make by bending this way and that, he gained new confidence, and the female dot fell in love with him.

The Dot and the Line was different from anything else Chuck had directed, because it included neither animals nor people. Chuck had already learned how to use animals' facial expressions to tell his stories. Bugs Bunny, Daffy Duck, or Pepé Le Pew needed only to raise an eyebrow or give the hint of a smile to indicate what Chuck was trying to say. Now he was capable of bringing human emotions to objects as simple as a dot and a line.

The ten-minute short film was such a hit that
Chuck won an Academy Award for it, in 1965.
A year later, Chuck reunited with Theodor Geisel
to direct a television version of Dr. Seuss's book
How the Grinch Stole Christmas!

Chuck's personal life took a sad turn in 1978, when Dorothy died at age seventy. His work life continued to thrive, however, with the release of *The Bugs Bunny/Road Runner Movie* in 1979. It featured several classic Looney Tunes cartoons and a series of chase scenes featuring the Road Runner and Wile E. Coyote. Bugs Bunny "hosted" the film in new scenes that Chuck helped write.

How the Grinch Stole Christmas

Dr. Seuss's classic book *How the Grinch Stole Christmas!* is often considered one of the best children's picture books of all time. It was first published in 1957. Nine years later, Chuck Jones worked with Theodor "Dr. Seuss" Geisel on an animated version of the book. The twenty-six-minute cartoon special was originally shown on CBS television in 1966, and it, too, is now considered a classic. It is still shown many times on television each Christmas season. Film star Boris Karloff—who had played Frankenstein in the movies—narrated the story and recorded the voice of the Grinch.

In 2000, *How the Grinch Stole Christmas!* was the first Dr. Seuss book to be adapted into a full-length film. And the story was retold in 2006 on Broadway in *Dr. Seuss' How the Grinch Stole Christmas! The Musical.*

In 1983, Chuck married Marian Dern, who once had interviewed him for *TV Guide* magazine. Chuck and Marian enjoyed traveling, and visited Europe, Australia, Japan, Mexico, and Canada together.

In 1985, Chuck's work was featured in an exhibition at the Museum of Modern Art in

New York City. And in 1992, *What's Opera, Doc?* became the first cartoon short ever added to the National Film Registry for its cultural and historical importance. *What's Opera, Doc?*

had been made in 1957. Sometimes referred to as "Kill the Wabbit," the cartoon follows Elmer Fudd as he chases Bugs Bunny through the stories and sets of several operas. The music was based on an opera written by classical composer Richard Wagner. The songs are sung by Arthur Q. Bryan, the voice of Elmer Fudd, and Mel Blanc, who was the voice of Bugs Bunny.

Mel Blanc (1908–1989)

Born Melvin Jerome Blank in San Francisco, California, Mel Blanc began his career in radio when he was just nineteen years old. He eventually became the voice of Bugs Bunny, Daffy Duck, Porky Pig, Yosemite Sam, Tweety Bird, Foghorn Leghorn, the Tasmanian Devil, and many other characters in Warner Bros.' Looney Tunes cartoons.

Blanc was nicknamed "the Man of a Thousand Voices," and that wasn't much of an exaggeration—if at all. In cartoons alone, he was the voice of more than four hundred characters.

What's Opera, Doc? is considered to be one of the greatest cartoons—if not *the* greatest cartoon—of all time. It introduced generations of children to the world of classical music. And it is considered to be the masterpiece of Chuck's career.

CHAPTER 8
From Hare to Eternity

In 1996, at the age of eighty-three, Chuck received an honorary Oscar at the Academy Awards for his lifetime achievements in animation. Chuck's appearance drew a rousing ovation from the crowd.

The Academy Awards

The Academy Awards, now called the Oscars, are the film industry's most important awards. Each year, the Academy of Motion Picture Arts and Sciences honors the year's best movies, directors, actors, artists, and technicians. It's the biggest night of the year for many people in the movie industry.

The Academy Awards first were presented in 1929. In 2013, the awards ceremony officially changed its name to the Oscars. "Oscar" is the nickname of the 13.5-inch gold statuette presented to each winner. In his lifetime, Chuck Jones won two Oscars, worked on two additional films that won Oscars, and worked on six others that were nominated.

Many directors, actors, and modern animators in Hollywood had grown up watching the Looney Tunes and Merrie Melodies cartoons. Matt Groening (who helped create *The Simpsons*) and John Lasseter (whose *Toy Story* in 1995 was the first full-length computer-animated feature) credit Chuck with inspiring their work.

John Lasseter and Matt Groening

In 1997, *From Hare to Eternity* was the last cartoon that Chuck Jones directed. In it, Bugs Bunny and Yosemite Sam are both interested in finding the same treasure.

When Chuck's directing days were over, he hardly stopped telling stories. In fact, he became very good at it. While he may not have been making movies with Bugs, Pepé, or Wile E. Coyote, he gladly shared his knowledge about them with fans, other animators, and journalists. He became a valuable source about what has come to be called the Golden Age of Animation.

In 2001, he was inducted into the Animation
Hall of Fame in Los Angeles.

When Warner Bros. closed its animation department in 1963 (it has since been reopened), the company destroyed existing cels—original illustrations—just to free up some space. Collectors and historians had lost many valuable pieces of animation art. Chuck spent time during his later years re-creating many of the cels from his days with Leon Schlesinger Productions and Warner Bros. They were sold or donated to charity.

Late in his life, Chuck Jones still could have turned on the television almost any day of the week and found a channel playing classic Looney Tunes or Merrie Melodies cartoons. That probably would have surprised anybody who had worked at Termite Terrace.

"What we . . . hoped was that our cartoons would have a life expectancy of four or five years," Chuck wrote, "because in those simple yet wonderfully creative years before television, we made films solely for theatrical release." No one could have predicted the enduring popularity those short films would still have so many decades later.

Chuck died of heart failure at age eighty-nine in 2002, but more than three hundred of his films—as cartoons—live on. His characters are often still found on television, clothing, and toys. In 2012, animation professionals celebrated what would have been Chuck's one hundredth birthday. And in January 2015, an exhibition called "What's Up, Doc? The Animation Art of Chuck Jones" closed a six-month run at New York's Museum of the Moving Image.

Chuck certainly was not thinking of such a lasting impact when he directed his cartoons for Warner Bros. Since shorts were originally shown with many different features, including romantic comedies, murder mysteries, and westerns, he had no way of knowing who his audience would be in the theaters. And it never seemed to matter. Instead, the directors, writers, and animators simply thought that if *they* laughed, the audience would, too. "We weren't making them for kids, or for adults," Chuck said. "We were making them for ourselves."

Chuck could see himself in Bugs Bunny, Road Runner, Wile E. Coyote, Daffy Duck, Pepé Le Pew, or any of the many other characters he created or shaped for Warner Bros.

"Those characters are extensions of myself: what I am or what I want to be," Chuck said.

Indeed, Chuck Jones was a little bit of all of them.

Timeline of Chuck Jones's Life

1912	Born September 21 in Spokane, Washington
1927	Leaves high school to attend Chouinard Art Institute
1933	Marries Dorothy Webster
1935	Goes to work for Leon Schlesinger Productions, which eventually was bought by Warner Bros.
1937	Daughter, Linda, is born
1938	Directs his first feature, *The Night Watchman*
1943	Begins working with Theodor Geisel (Dr. Seuss) on educational cartoons for US soldiers
1950	Two of his films—*For Scent-imental Reasons* and *So Much for So Little*—each wins an Oscar at the Academy Awards
1963	Begins to work at MGM
1965	Wins an Academy Award for Best Animated Cartoon (*The Dot and the Line*)
1966	Directs television adaptation of Dr. Seuss's *How the Grinch Stole Christmas!*
1978	Dorothy Webster Jones dies at seventy
1985	Work is featured at the Museum of Modern Art in New York City
1992	*What's Opera, Doc?* added to the National Film Registry
1996	Receives an honorary Oscar at the Academy Awards
2001	Inducted into the Animation Hall of Fame in Los Angeles
2002	Dies at eighty-nine on February 22

Timeline of the World

1912	The cruise ship *Titanic* sinks on its first voyage
1914	World War I begins in Europe and lasts until 1918
1920	The Nineteenth Amendment gives women the right to vote in the United States
1928	The first television station in the US begins operating in Wheaton, Maryland
1932	Franklin Delano Roosevelt is elected president of the United States for the first of a record four terms
1938	The first Superman comic book is published
1939	World War II begins in Europe and lasts until 1945
1941	The United States officially enters World War II after Japan attacks Pearl Harbor in Hawaii
1947	Jackie Robinson of the Brooklyn Dodgers becomes the first black player in the modern era of Major League Baseball
1951	Color television is introduced to the public
1955	Disneyland opens in Anaheim, California
1969	Neil Armstrong becomes the first man to walk on the moon
1976	Steve Wozniak and Steve Jobs start Apple Computers
1981	MTV starts broadcasting music videos
2001	The World Trade Center in New York City and the Pentagon in Arlington County, Virginia, are attacked by al-Qaeda on September 11

Bibliography

* Books for young readers

Adamson, Joe. *Bugs Bunny: Fifty Years and Only One Grey Hare*.
New York: Henry Holt and Company, 1990.

Beck, Jerry. *The 100 Greatest Looney Tunes Cartoons*. San Rafael, CA:
Insight Editions, 2010.

Farago, Andrew. *Looney Tunes Treasury*. Philadelphia: Running Press,
2010.

Jones, Chuck. *Chuck Amuck: The Life and Times of an Animated
Cartoonist*. New York: Farrar Straus Giroux, 1989.

Jones, Chuck. *Chuck Reducks: Drawing from the Fun Side of Life*.
New York: Warner Books, 1996.

* Jones, Chuck. *Daffy Duck for President*. Burbank, CA: Warner Bros. Worldwide Publishing, 1997.

Kenner, Hugh. *Chuck Jones: A Flurry of Drawings*. Berkeley: University of California Press, 1994.

Maltin, Leonard. *Of Mice and Magic: A History of American Animated Cartoons*. New York: Plume, 1987.

* Steffens, Bradley, and Robyn M. Weaver. *Cartoonists*. San Diego: Lucent Books, 2000.